To Barbara,

Enjoy -
Ann Lind

flights
of fancy

HarperCollins*Publishers*

Library of Congress Catalog Card Number: 91-55263
ISBN: 0-06-016655-X

Printed in Singapore
First Edition
1   2   3   4   5   6   7   8   9   10

Edited by Sheila Buff
Designed by Dirk Kaufman
Produced by Smallwood and Stewart, New York City

Permissions and copyright notices appear on pages 94 and 95.

INTRODUCTION

O to mount again where erst I haunted;

Where the old red hills are bird-enchanted. . . .

Robert Louis Stevenson

From as far back as anyone knows, birds have been a subject of mankind's wonder. Depictions of recognizable bird species have been found in paleolithic cave paintings nearly 20,000 years old. But until very recently in human history, much about them was deeply mysterious. Where did they go when they flew off into the sky? Why did they disappear for months on end? Being so varied, puzzling, and seemingly magical with their ability to fly, birds, not surprisingly, have rich literary and religious associations in all cultures, which appear in mythology and art.

In early civilizations, deities were frequently endowed with the qualities of birds that seemed best to portray grace, beauty, and power. The gods of the ancient Egyptians, for example, were often depicted with the bodies of men and the heads of birds—the sun gods Ra and Horus sported the heads of falcons; the god of wisdom, Thoth, is shown with the head of an ibis, a sacred bird among the Egyptians. Some Native Americans believed the mythical thunderbird to be the guardian of fire and the wise protector of humanity. The wily raven figures in many creation stories in the role of a mischievous trickster.

Bird symbolism has also played a significant part in Judeo-Christian religions. To learn whether the waters of the great flood had receded, Noah sent out a dove, which returned bearing an olive sprig in its bill. The dove has been a symbol of peace and purity ever since. The European goldfinch has an affinity for the seeds of the thistle plant, whose thorns in turn are associated with the Passion of Christ; thus this bird is often a symbol of the Passion itself and also of the Virgin Mary. Even angels are given the wings of birds.

Birds also figure extensively in the world's folk literature of legends, myths, superstitions, songs, and fairy tales. Persian tales speak of the mythical roc, a gigantic bird capable of carrying off an elephant. The phoenix, a vivid symbol of death and resurrection, which still today resonates power-fully with us, was first recorded in the fifth century B.C. by the Greek historian Herodotus. According to legend there is only one phoenix, which lives for a hundred years. At the end of its century, it is consumed in flames, only to arise reborn from the ashes.

Birds continue to inspire literature and art. In current literature, as in times of old, birds evoke a myriad of emotions — as is evident in the poetry of Robert Penn Warren, the observations of naturalist Sue Hubbell, and the fiction by E. B. White collected here. The effortless flights of birds is a fre-quent symbol of freedom and grace. The cheerful singing and frenetic activ-ity of birds in springtime evokes a powerful sense of reawakening and joy in some, and feelings of sadness and longing in others. In some of the best writing about birds, a sense of wonder tinged with awe is suggested, wonder that birds exist in so many ways, with such beauty, and with such amazing natural abilities.

In many ways, birds are like ourselves in microcosm, stripped to the essentials and made evident. The birds court their mates hopefully; they la-bor long to build and defend their homes; and they raise their young with selfless dedication.

Sheila Buff Spring 1991

The great flock swept before me in a mad rush of swishing, flashing wings, outstretched necks and heads, rigid legs. In an instant the visible world was filled with a confused, careening mass of pink birds; in another the roar of sound had ceased, the hurtling bodies, the confusion of wings had disappeared.

Robert Porter Allen
The Flame Birds

Merry, merry sparrow!
Under leaves so green
A happy blossom
Sees you swift as arrow
Seek your cradle narrow
Near my bosom. . . .

William Blake

THE WINDHOVER

I caught this morning morning's minion, king-
dom of daylight's dauphin, dapple-dawn-drawn falcon, in
his riding
Of the rolling level underneath him steady air, and striding
High there, how he rung upon the rein of a wimpling wing
In his ecstasy!

Gerard Manley Hopkins

Out of the cradle endlessly rocking,
Out of the mocking-bird's throat, the
musical shuttle. . . .

Walt Whitman

The sun, as it rose, tinged the quick-silver of the creeks and the gleaming slime itself with flame. The curlew, who had been piping their mournful plaints since long before the light, flew now from weed-bank to weed-bank. The widgeon, who had slept on water, came whistling their double notes, like whistles from a Christmas cracker. The mallard toiled from land, against the wind. The redshanks scuttled and

prodded like mice. A cloud of tiny dunlin, more compact than starlings, turned in the air with the noise of a train. The black-guard of crows rose from the pine trees on the dunes with merry cheers. Shore birds of every sort populated the tide line, filling it with business and beauty.

T. H. White
The Once and Future King

"What is a Scarlet Tanager?" mused the child, whose
consciousness had flown with the wonderful appari-
tion on wings of ecstasy; but the bees hummed on,
the scent of the flowers floated by, the sunbeam pas-
sed across the greensward, and there was no reply —
nothing but the echo of a mute appeal to Nature,
stirring the very depths with an inward thrill.

Elliot Coues
Birds of the Colorado Valley

Early summer days are a jubilee time for birds. In the fields, around the house, in the barn, in the woods, in the swamp—everywhere love and songs and nests and eggs. From the edge of the woods, the white-throated sparrow (which must come all the way from Boston) calls, "Oh, Peabody, Peabody, Peabody!" On an apple bough, the phoebe teeters and wags its tail and says, "Phoebe, phoe-bee!" The song sparrow, who knows how brief and lovely life is, says, "Sweet, sweet, sweet interlude; sweet, sweet, sweet interlude." If you enter the barn, the swallows swoop down from their nests and scold. "Cheeky, cheeky!" they say.

E. B. White
Charlotte's Web

Upon the brimming water among the stones
Are nine-and-fifty swans.

But now they drift on the still water,
Mysterious, beautiful;
Among what rushes will they build,
By what lake's edge or pool
Delight men's eyes when I awake some day
To find they have flown away?

William Butler Yeats
The Wild Swans at Coole

t had honored our clearing
with its presence because
even a royal bird must preen
wind-ruffled feathers. Carefully it ten-
ded its wings and breast, then fluffed
and settled and posed on the treetop.
Its broad, heavy breast testified to its
great flight power. Its feathers were
like fresh snow. Even its beak and feet
were pale. Its pupils were circles of
black fire, and the dark dotted lines on
its back and wings, the chevron marks
on its primaries, were like ermine tails
on the coronation robes of nobility.

Helen Blackburn Hoover
The Long–Shadowed Forest

Time, happily for them, is no object; but this at first sight one
would hardly guess, their movements being always precise,
busy, and preoccupied. It is only when one has watched a little
party hurrying along for full half a mile in a direct line, as
though upon some urgent business, suddenly stop and all go to
sleep, or suddenly turn and go off in another direction, or
come back upon some equally urgent call, that one begins
to realise that their business is not always so important
as it looks.

Edward Wilson
Journals

My musical friend, at whose
house I am now visiting, has
tried all the owls that are his
near neighbors with a pitch-pipe
set at concert-pitch, and finds
they all hoot in B flat. He will
examine the nightingales
next spring.

Gilbert White
The Natural History of Selborne

Seagulls

... slim yachts of the element.

Robinson Jeffers
Pelicans

he diversity in the appearance of birds is as fantastic as their range in size. Compare a Penguin with its flightless seal-like flippers to the Wandering Albatross with its eleven-foot sails. Or contrast the homely, hairy-looking Kiwi, devoid of wings, to a Peacock or a Bird of Paradise! . . . Bills show every imaginable adaptation; there are the thick seed-cracking bills of Finches, pruning-shear bills of Crossbills, slender probing bills of Snipe and Hummingbirds, chisel bills of Woodpeckers, spear bills of Herons, saw-toothed bills of Mergansers, shovel bills of Ducks, hooked beaks of Hawks and Owls, and the huge colorful probosci of Toucans.

Roger Tory Peterson
How to Know the Birds

THE EAGLE

He clasps the crag with crooked hands;
Close to the sun in lonely lands,
Ringed with the azure world, he stands.

The wrinkled sea beneath him crawls;
He watches from his mountain walls,
And like a thunderbolt he falls.

Alfred, Lord Tennyson

Have you ever observed a humming-bird moving about in an aërial dance among the flowers — a living prismatic gem that changes its colour with every change of position — how in turning it catches the sunshine on its burnished neck and gorget plumes — green and gold and flame-coloured, the beams changing to visible flakes as they fall, dissolving into nothing, to be succeeded by others and yet others? In its exquisite form, its changeful splendour, its swift motions and intervals of aërial suspension, it is a creature of such fairy-like loveliness as to mock all description.

W. H. Hudson
Green Mansions

ut of the dimming sky a speck appeared, then another, and another. It was the starlings going to roost. They gathered deep in the distance, flock sifting into flock, and strayed towards me, transparent and whirling, like smoke. They seemed to unravel as they flew, lengthening in curves, like a loosened skein. I didn't move; they flew directly over my head for half an hour. The flight extended like a fluttering banner, an unfurled oriflamme, in either direction as far as I could see. Each individual bird bobbed and knitted up and down in the flight at apparent random, for no known reason except that that's how starlings fly, yet all remained perfectly spaced. The flocks each tapered at either end from a rounded middle, like an eye. Over my head I heard a sound of beaten air, like a million shook rugs, a muffled whuff. Into the woods they sifted without shifting a twig, right through the crowns of trees, intricate and rushing, like wind.

Annie Dillard
Pilgrim at Tinker Creek

41

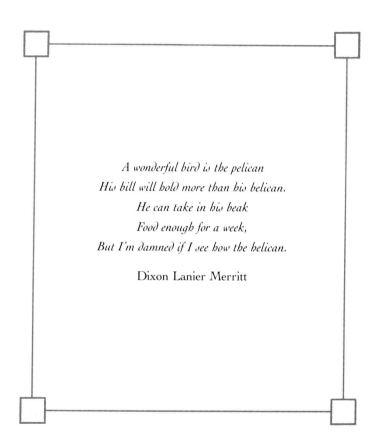

A wonderful bird is the pelican
His bill will hold more than his belican.
He can take in his beak
Food enough for a week,
But I'm damned if I see how the helican.

Dixon Lanier Merritt

A bird's-nest suggests design, and yet it seems almost haphazard; the result of a kind of madness, yet with method in it. The hole the woodpecker drills for its cell is to the eye a perfect circle, and the rim of most nests is as true as that of a cup. The circle and the sphere exist in nature; they are mother forms and hold all other forms. They

are easily attained; they are spontaneous and inevitable.
The bird models her nest about her own breast; she turns
round and round in it, and its circular character results as a
matter of course. Angles, right lines, measured precision, so
characteristic of the works of man, are rarely met with in
organic nature.

John Burroughs
Ways of Nature

BIRD NOUNS OF ASSEMBLAGE

bouquet of pheasants

cast of hawks

charm of finches

clamor of rooks

commotion of coot

congregation of plover

exaltation of larks

fall of woodcock

gaggle of geese

murder of crows

murmuration of starlings

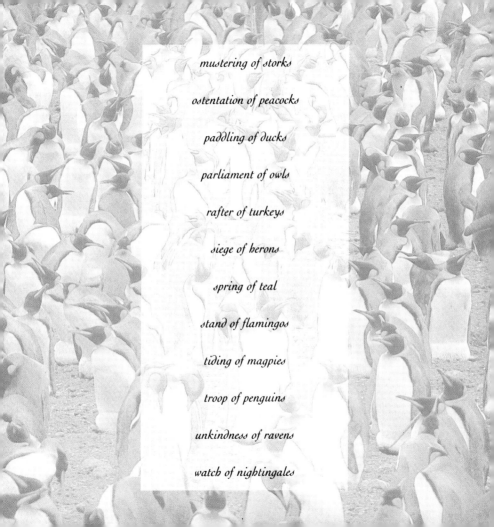

mustering of storks

ostentation of peacocks

paddling of ducks

parliament of owls

rafter of turkeys

siege of herons

spring of teal

stand of flamingos

tiding of magpies

troop of penguins

unkindness of ravens

watch of nightingales

Indigo buntings are small but
emphatic birds. They believe
that they own the place, and it is
hard to ignore their claim.

Sue Hubbell
A Country Year

THERE ONCE WAS A PUFFIN

Oh, there once was a puffin
Just the shape of a muffin,
And he lived on an island
In the
      deep
          Blue
              Sea.

He ate little fishes
Which were most delicious
And he had them for breakfast
And he had
      them
          for
              tea.

But the poor little puffin
He couldn't play nothin',
For he hadn't anybody
To play
      with
          at
              all.

So he sat on his island
And he cried for a while, and
He felt very lonesome
And he
        felt
            very
                small.

Then along came the fishes
And they said, "If you wishes
You can have us for playmates
Instead
        of
            for
                tea."

So they all play together
In all sorts of weather;
And the puffin eats pancakes
Like you
        and
            like
                me.

Florence Page Jacques

51

Sweet are the sounds that mingle from afar,
Heard by calm lakes, as peeps the folding star,
Where the duck dabbles 'mid the rustling sedge,
And feeding pike starts from the waters edge,
Or the swan stirs the reeds, his neck and bill
Wetting, that drip upon the water still;
And heron, as resounds the trodden shore,
Shoots upward, darting his long neck before.

William Wordsworth
An Evening Walk

To hear an Oriole sing
May be a common thing—
Or only a divine . . .

Emily Dickinson

I never for a day gave up listening to the songs of our birds, or watching their peculiar habits, or delineating them in the best way that I could.

John James Audubon
Journals

Gordonia Pubescens

It's a warm wind, the west wind,
full of birds' cries. . . .

John Masefield

Why, ye tenants of the lake,
For me your wat'ry haunt forsake?
Tell me, fellow creatures, why
At my presence thus you fly?
Why disturb your social joys,
Parent, filial, kindred ties? —
Common friend to you and me,
Nature's gifts to all are free:
Peaceful keep your dimpling wave,
Busy feed, or wanton lave;
Or, beneath the sheltering rock,
Bide the surging billow's shock . . .

Robert Burns
On Scaring Some Waterfowl

Then the little Hiawatha
Learned of every bird its language,
Learned their names and all their secrets,
How they built their nests in Summer,
Where they hid themselves in Winter,
Talked with them whene'er he met them. . . .

Henry Wadsworth Longfellow
The Song of Hiawatha

Remember that the most beautiful things in the world are the
most useless; peacocks and lilies
for instance.

John Ruskin
The Stones of Venice

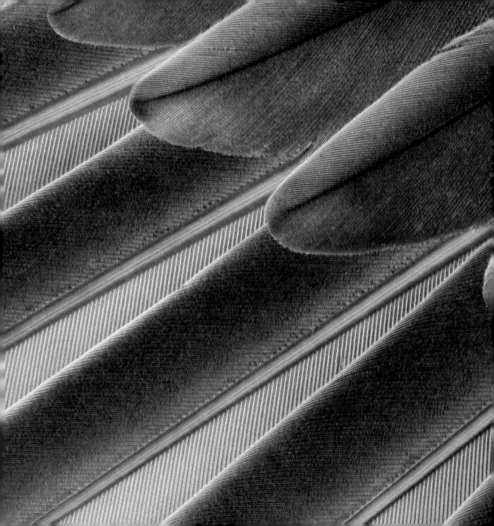

The birds — are they worth remembering?
Is flight a wonder and one wingtip a
space marvel?
When will man know what birds know?

Carl Sandburg
Wingtip

Find a fall, or cascade, or rushing
rapid, anywhere upon a clear stream,
and there you will surely find its com-
plementary Ouzel, flitting about in
the spray, diving in foaming eddies,
whirling like a leaf among beaten foam-
balls; ever vigorous and enthusiastic,
yet self-contained, and neither seeking
nor shunning your company.

John Muir
The Mountains of California

I like to think that the appeal of birds lies in their incomparably vivid representation of life. It is as if the essential principle had been isolated in these creatures to display its attributes most pointedly and most movingly. Consider the cedar waxwing's refinement of sculpture and creamy-consistency of hue. Could a conscious artistic inspiration have wrought with greater sureness?

Charlton Ogburn, Jr.
Atlantic Naturalist

The crow is a generous bird;
he has the true social instinct.

John Burroughs
Under the Apple-Trees

March 27, 1842. The little hawks have just come out to play, like butterflies rising one above the other in endless alterna-

tion. . . . They swoop from side to side in the broad basin of the tree-tops. . . . *April 1, 1852.* As I come over the turnpike, the song-sparrow's jingle comes up from every part of the meadow, as native as the tinkling rills or the blossoms of the spirea. Its *cheep* is like the sound of opening buds. . . . *June 22, 1853.* . . . I hear the wood-thrush singing his evening lay. This is the only bird whose note affects me like music, affects the flow and tenor of my thought, my fancy, and imagination. It lifts and exhila-rates me. . . . *January 8, 1854.* Stood within a rod of a downy woodpecker on an apple-tree. How curious and exciting the blood-red spot on its hind head! . . . *November 28, 1858.* "Hear! hear!" screamed the jay from a neighboring tree, where I had heard a tittering for some time, "winter has a concentrated and nutty kernel, if you know where to look for it.". . .

December 12, 1858. I see an immense flock of snow buntings, I think the largest I ever saw. . . . Like a snowstorm, they come rushing down from the north. . . . *March 2, 1859.* The bluebird comes, and with his warble drills the ice, and sets free

the rivers and ponds and frozen ground. . . . The sharp whistle of the blackbird, too, is heard like single sparks, or a shower of them, shot up from the swamp and seen against the dark winter in the rear.

Henry David Thoreau
Journals of Henry David Thoreau

I examined many specimens in the different islands, and in each the respective kind was *alone* present. These birds agree in general plumage, structure, and habits; so that the different species replace each other in the economy of the different islands. These species are not characterized by the markings on the plumage alone, but likewise by the size and form of the bill, and other differences. I have stated, that in the thirteen species of ground-finches, a nearly perfect gradation may be traced, from a beak extraordinarily thick, to one so fine, that it may be compared to that of a warbler. I very much suspect, that certain members of the series are confined to different islands; therefore, if the collection had been made on any *one* island, it would not have presented so perfect a gradation. It is clear, that if several islands have each their peculiar species of the same genera, when these are placed together, they will have a wide range of character. But there is no space in this work to enter on this curious subject.

Charles Darwin
The Voyage

It was my thirtieth year to heaven
Woke to my hearing from harbour and neighbour wood
And the mussel pooled and the heron
Priested shore.

Dylan Thomas
Poem in October

Flamingos in flight resemble no other
bird known to me. With legs and necks
fully outstretched, and the comparatively
small wings set half-way between bill
and toes, they look as if they might fly
backward or forward with equal ease.

Frank M. Chapman
Camps and Cruises of an Ornithologist

BIRD CALL MNEMONICS

razorbill . . . *Hey Al!*

oldsquaw . . . *Owl omelet*

sooty tern . . . *Wide-a-wake*

greater yellowlegs . . . *Dear! dear! dear!*

willow ptarmigan . . . *Tobacco, tobacco*

olive-sided flycatcher . . . *Hic! three beers*

blue jay . . . *Thief, thief!*

tufted titmouse . . . *Peter, peter, peter*

Carolina wren . . . *Teakettle, teakettle, teakettle, tea*

American robin . . . *Cheerily, cheerily, cheer up*

yellow-throated vireo . . . *Three eight*

chestnut-sided warbler . . . *I wish to see Miss Beecher*

Connecticut warbler . . . *Sugar-tweet, sugar-tweet, sugar-tweet*

yellow warbler . . . *Sweet sweet sweet I'm so sweet*

ovenbird . . . *Tea-cher, tea-CHER, TEA-CHER, TEA-CHER*

northern cardinal . . . *What cheer, cheer, cheer*

rufous-sided towhee . . . *Drink your tea-a-a!*

California quail . . . *Chicago!*

warbling vireo . . . *When I see one I shall seize one and I'll squeeze it 'til it SQUIRTS!*

barred owl . . . *Who cooks for you, who cooks for allll?*

eastern meadowlark . . . *Spring of the year!*

American goldfinch . . . *potato chip, potato chip*

white-throated sparrow . . . *Oh sweet Canada, Canada, Canada*

SANDPIPERS

Ten miles of flat land along the sea.
Sandland where the salt water kills the sweet potatoes.
Homes for sandpipers — the script of their feet is on the sea shingles —
they write in the morning, it is gone at noon — they write at noon, it
is gone at night.
Pity the land, the sea, the ten mile flats, pity anything but the sand-
pipers' wire legs and feet.

Carl Sandburg

The loons of Lac la Croix are part of the vast solitudes, the hundreds of rocky islands, the long reaches of the lake toward the Maligne, the Snake, and the Namakon. My memory is full of their calling: in the morning when the white horses of the mists are galloping out of the bays, at midday when their long, lazy bugling is part of the calm, and at dusk when their music joins with that of the hermit thrushes and the wilderness is going to sleep.

Sigurd F. Olson
The Singing Wilderness

Yon bird is but her messenger,
The moon is but her silver car;
Yea! sun and moon are sent by her,
And every wistful waiting star.

Richard Le Gallienne
Song

It was only a bird call at evening, unidentified,
As I came from the spring with water, across the rocky back-pasture;
But so still I stood sky above was not stiller the sky in pail-water.

Years pass, all places and faces fade, some people have died,
And I stand in a far land, the evening still, and am at last sure
That I miss more that stillness at bird-call than some things that
were to fail later.

Robert Penn Warren,
Ornithology in a World of Flux

INDEX TO ILLUSTRATED SPECIES

63	red-headed weaver (*Anaplectes rubriceps*)
64	blue (Indian) peacock (*Pavo cristatus*)
68–69	American dipper (*Cinclus mexicanus*)
71	cedar waxwing (*Bombycilla cedrorum*)
72–73	American crow (*Corvus brachyrhyncos*)
74	eastern bluebird (*Sialia sialis*)
75	(top) blue jay (*Cyanocitta cristata*)
75	(bottom) downy woodpecker (*Picoides pubescens*)
77	Darwin's finch (family Geospiza)
79	great blue heron (*Ardea herodias*)
81	greater flamingo (*Phoenicopterus ruber*)
84	dunlin (*Calidrus alpina*)
85	sanderling (*Calidris alba*)
87	common loon (*Gavia immer*)
88	Canada goose (*Branta canadensis*)
90–91	red-winged blackbird (*Agelaius nhoeniceus*)
96	European starling (*Sturnus vulgaris*)

PHOTO CREDITS

Michael Baytoff	1, 14–15, 84, 85, 90–91, 96;
Barbara A. Brundege	Jacket background and jacket back, 58–59, 82–83;
Comstock	Jacket front, 13, 17, 21, 22, 25, 26, 35, 40, 63, 64, 68–69, 77;
ET Archive	42;
Imagery	32–33, 45, 50–51, 52–53, 66–67;
Dirk Kaufman	5;
Wayne Lankinen	48, 71, 74;
C. Allan Morgan	18–19, 30;
The New-York Historical Society	57;
Ron Sanford	60–61, 79;
Gregory L. Scott	55, 75 (top and bottom), 87;
Norm Smith	88;
Vireo	10–11, 37, 39, 81;
Art Wolfe	28, 44, 46–47, 73.

BIOGRAPHIES

Allen, Robert Porter (1905–63), American ornithologist and author

Audubon, John James (1785–1851), American bird painter

Blake, William (1757–1827), English poet and artist

Burns, Robert (1759–96), Scottish poet

Burroughs, John (1837–1921), American nature writer

Chapman, Frank (1864–1945), American ornithologist

Coues, Elliot (1842–99), American ornithologist

Darwin, Charles (1809–82), English naturalist

Dickinson, Emily (1830–86), American poet

Dillard, Annie (b. 1945), American poet and essayist

Hoover, Helen Blackburn (1910–84), American nature writer

Hopkins, Gerard Manley (1844–89), English poet

Hubbell, Sue (b. 1935), American essayist and beekeeper

Hudson, W. H. (1841–1922), English novelist and naturalist

Jacques, Florence Page (1890–1972), American nature writer

Jeffers, Robinson (1887–1962), American poet

Le Gallienne, Richard (1866–1947), English journalist and writer

Longfellow, Henry Wadsworth (1807–82), American poet

Masefield, John (1878–1967), English poet; poet laureate 1930–67

Merritt, Dixon Lanier (1879–1972), American editor, historian, and poet

Muir, John (1838–1914), American naturalist and writer

Ogburn, Charlton, Jr. (b. 1911), American naturalist and writer

Olson, Sigurd F. (b. 1899), American naturalist, conservationist, and writer

Peterson, Roger Tory (b. 1908), American bird painter and writer

Ruskin, John (1819–1900), English art critic

Sandburg, Carl (1878–1967), American poet and biographer

Stevenson, Robert Louis (1850–94), English novelist, poet, and essayist

Tennyson, Alfred, Lord (1809–92), English poet; poet laureate 1850–92

Thomas, Dylan (1914–53), Welsh poet and writer

Thoreau, Henry David (1817–62), American philosopher, naturalist, and poet

Warren, Robert Penn (1905–89), American novelist and poet

White, E. B. (1899–1985), American essayist

White, Gilbert (1720–93), English clergyman and naturalist

White, T. H. (1906–64), English writer and poet

Whitman, Walt (1819–92), American poet

Wilson, Edward (1872–1912), English naturalist and Antarctic explorer

Wordsworth, William (1770–1850), English poet; poet laureate 1843–50

Yeats, William Butler (1865–1939), Irish poet and dramatist

ACKNOWLEDGMENTS

Excerpt from *Pilgrim at Tinker Creek* by Annie Dillard. Copyright © 1974 by Annie Dillard. Reprinted by permission of HarperCollins Publishers.

Excerpt from *The Long-Shadowed Forest* by Helen Blackburn Hoover, reprinted by permission of W.W. Norton & Company, Inc. Copyright © 1963 by Helen Hoover and Adrian Hoover. Copyright renewed 1991.

A Country Year: Living the Questions by Sue Hubbell. Copyright © 1983, 1984, 1985, 1986 by Sue Hubbell. Reprinted by permission of Random House, Inc.

Excerpt from *The Atlantic Naturalist* by Charlton Ogburn, Jr. Copyright © 1953 by the Audobon Naturalist Society of the Central Atlantic States. Reprinted with permission of the Audobon Naturalist Society of the Central Atlantic States.

Excerpt from *How to Know the Birds* by Roger Tory Peterson. Copyright © 1949 by Roger Tory Peterson. Reprinted by permission of New American Library, a division of Penguin Books U.S.A. Inc.

"Sandpipers" by Carl Sandburg from *Smoke and Steel*. Copyright © 1920 by Harcourt Brace Jovanovich, Inc. and renewed 1948 by Carl Sandburg, reprinted by permission of the publisher.

"Poem in October" by Dylan Thomas from *Poems of Dylan Thomas*. Copyright © 1945 by the Trustees for the Copyrights of Dylan Thomas. First printed in *Poetry*. Reprinted by permission of New Directions Publishing Corporation.

"Ornithology in a World of Flux," by Robert Penn Warren, is from *Selected Poems 1923–1975* by Robert Penn Warren. Copyright © 1976 by Robert Penn Warren. Reprinted by permission of Random House, Inc.

Excerpt from *Charlotte's Web* by E. B. White. Copyright © 1952 by E. B. White. Text copyright renewed © 1980 by E. B. White. Reprinted by permission of HarperCollins Publishers.

The Once and Future King by T. H. White. Copyright © 1958 by T. H. White. Renewed 1986 Lloyd's Bank. Reprinted by permission of The Putnam Publishing Group.

"The Wild Swans at Coole," by William Butler Yeats, is from *The Poems of W. B. Yeats: A New Edition*, edited by Richard J. Finneran. Copyright © 1919 by Macmillan Publishing Company, renewed 1947 by Bertha Georgie Yeats. Reprinted with permission of Macmillan Publishing Company.